Table of Contents

For All Students 2

Kinds of Questions 9

Practice Test—Reading & Language Arts 15

Practice Test—Basic Skills 27

Practice Test—Math 34

Practice Test—Social Studies 39

Practice Test—Science 41

Final Test—Reading & Language Arts 43

Final Test—Basic Skills 53

Final Test—Math 65

Final Test—Social Studies 73

Final Test—Science 75

Answer Key 77

Taking Standardized Tests

No matter what grade you're in, this is information you can use to prepare for standardized tests. Here is what you'll find:

- Test-taking tips and strategies to use on test day and year-round.
- Important terms to know for Language Arts, Reading, Math, Science, and Social Studies.
- A checklist of skills to complete to help you understand what you need to know in Language Arts, Reading Comprehension, Writing, and Math.
- General study/homework tips.

By opening this book, you've already taken your first step towards test success. The rest is easy—all you have to do is get started!

What You Need to Know

There are many things you can do to increase your test success. Here's a list of tips to keep in mind when you take standardized tests—and when you study for them, too.

Keep up with your school work. One way you can succeed in school and on tests is by studying and doing your homework regularly. Studies show that you remember only about one-fifth of what you memorize the night before a test. That's one good reason not to try to learn it all at once! Keeping up with your work throughout the year will help you remember the material better. You also won't be as tired or nervous as if you try to learn everything at once.

Feel your best. One of the ways you can do your best on tests and in school is to make sure your body is ready. To do this, get a good night's sleep each night and eat a healthy breakfast (not sugary cereal that will leave you tired by the middle of the morning). An egg or a milkshake with yogurt and fresh fruit will give you lasting energy. Also, wear comfortable clothes, maybe your lucky shirt or your favorite color on test day. It can't hurt, and it may even keep you relax.

Be prepared. Do practice questions and learn about how standardized tests are organized. Books like this one will help you know what to expect when you take a standardized test.

When you are taking the test, follow the directions. It is important to listen carefully to the directions your teacher gives and to read the written instructions carefully. Words like *not*, *none*, *rarely*, *never*, and *always* are very important in test directions and questions. You may want to circle words like these.

Look at each page carefully before you start answering. In school you usually read a passage and then answer questions about it. But when you take a test, it's helpful to follow a different order.

If you are taking a Reading test, first read the directions. Then, read the *questions* before you read the passage. This way you will know exactly what kind of information to look for as you read. Next, read the passage carefully. Finally, answer the questions.

On math and science tests, look at the labels on graphs and charts. Think about what each graph or chart shows. Questions often will ask you to draw conclusions about the information.

Manage your time. *Time management* means using your time wisely on a test so that you can finish as much of it as possible and do your best. Look over the test or the parts that you are allowed to do at one time. Sometimes you may want to do the easier parts first. This way, if you run out of time before you finish, you will have completed a good chunk of the work.

For tests that have a time limit, notice what time it is when the test begins and figure out when you need to stop. Check a few times as you work through the test to be sure you are making good progress and not spending too much time on any particular section.

You don't have to keep up with everyone else. You may notice other students in the class finishing before you do. Don't worry about this. Everyone works at a different pace. Just keep going, trying not to spend too long on any one question.

Fill in answer sheets properly. Even if you know every answer on a test, you won't do well unless you enter the answers correctly on the answer sheet.

Fill in the entire bubble, but don't spend too much time making it perfect. Make your mark dark, but not so dark that it goes through the paper! And be sure you only choose one answer for each question, even if you are not sure. If you choose two answers, both will be marked as wrong.

It's usually not a good idea to change your answers. Usually your first choice is the right one. Unless you realize that you misread the question, the directions, or some facts in a passage, it's usually safer to stay with your first answer. If you are pretty sure it's wrong, of course, go ahead and change it. Make sure you completely erase the first choice and neatly fill in your new choice.

Use context clues to figure out tough questions. If you come across a word or idea you don't understand, use context clues—the words in the sentences nearby— to help you figure out its meaning.

Sometimes it's good to guess. Should you guess when you don't know an answer on a test? That depends. If your teacher has made the test, usually you will score better if you answer as many questions as possible, even if you don't really know the answers.

On standardized tests, here's what to do to score your best. For each question, most of these tests let you choose from four or five answer choices. If you decide that a couple of answers are clearly wrong but you're still not sure about the answer, go ahead and make your best guess. If you can't narrow down the choices at all, then you may be better off skipping the question. Tests like these take away extra points for wrong answers, so it's better to leave them blank. Be sure you skip over the answer space for these questions on the answer sheet, though, so you don't fill in the wrong spaces.

Sometimes you should skip a question and come back to it later.

On many tests, you will score better if you answer more questions. This means that you should not spend too much time on any single question. Sometimes it gets tricky, though, keeping track of questions you skipped on your answer sheet.

If you want to skip a question because you don't know the answer, put a very light pencil mark next to the question in the test booklet. Try to choose an answer, even if you're not sure of it. Fill in the answer lightly on the answer sheet.

Check your work.
On a standardized test, you can't go ahead or skip back to another section of the test. But you may go back and review your answers on the section you just worked on if you have extra time.

First, scan your answer sheet. Make sure that you answered every question you could. Also, if you are using a bubble-type answer sheet, make sure that you filled in only one bubble for each question. Erase any extra marks on the page.

Finally—avoid test anxiety!
If you get nervous about tests, don't worry. *Test anxiety* happens to lots of good students. Being a little nervous actually sharpens your mind. But if you get very nervous about tests, take a few minutes to relax the night before or the day of the test. One good way to relax is to get some exercise, even if you just have time to stretch, shake out your fingers, and wiggle your toes. If you can't move around, it helps just to take a few slow, deep breaths and picture yourself doing a great job!

Terms to Know

Here's a list of terms that are good to know when taking standardized tests. Don't be worried if you see something new. You may not have learned it in school yet.

acute angle: an angle of less than 90°

adjective: a word that describes a noun (*yellow duckling, new bicycle*)

adverb: a word that describes a verb (*ran fast, laughing heartily*)

analogy: a comparison of the relationship between two or more otherwise unrelated things (*Carrot is to vegetable as banana is to fruit.*)

angle: the figure formed by two lines that start at the same point, usually shown in degrees **90°**

antonyms: words with opposite meanings (*big* and *small, young* and *old*)

area: the amount of space inside a flat shape, expressed in square units

article: a word such as *a, an,* or *the* that goes in front of a noun (*the chicken, an apple*)

cause/effect: the reason that something happens

character: a person in a story, book, movie, play, or TV show

compare/contrast: to tell what is alike and different about two or more things

compass rose: the symbol on a map that shows where North, South, East, and West are

conclusion: a logical decision you can make based on information from a reading selection or science experiment

congruent: equal in size or shape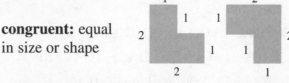

context clues: language and details in a piece of writing that can help you figure out difficult words and ideas

denominator: in a fraction, the number under the line; shows how many equal parts a whole has been divided into ($\frac{1}{2}, \frac{6}{7}$)

direct object: in a sentence, the person or thing that receives the action of a verb (*Jane hit the ball hard.*)

equation: in math, a statement where one set of numbers or values is equal to another set (*6 + 6 = 12, 4 x 5 = 20*)

factor: a whole number that can be divided exactly into another whole number (*1, 2, 3, 4, and 6 are all factors of 12.*)

genre: a category of literature that contains writing with common features (*drama, fiction, nonfiction, poetry*)

hypothesis: in science, the possible answer to a question; most science experiments begin with a hypothesis

indirect object: in a sentence, the noun or pronoun that tells to or for whom the action of the verb is done (*Louise gave a flower to her sister.*)

infer: to make an educated guess about a piece of writing, based on information contained in the selection and what you already know

main idea: the most important idea or message in a writing selection

map legend: the part of a map showing symbols that represent natural or human-made objects

noun: a person, place, or thing (*president, underground, train*)

numerator: in a fraction, the number above the line; shows how many equal parts are to be taken from the denominator ($\frac{3}{4}, \frac{1}{5}$)

operation: in math, tells what must be done to numbers in an equation (such as add, subtract, multiply, or divide)

parallel: lines or rays that, if extended, could never intersect

percent: fraction of a whole that has been divided into 100 parts, usually expressed with % sign ($\frac{5}{100} = 5\%$)

perimeter: distance around an object or shape

Perimeter =
3 + 3 + 3 + 3 = 12 ft.

perpendicular: lines or rays that intersect to form a 90° (right) angle

90°

predicate: in a sentence, the word or words that tell what the subject does, did, or has (*The fuzzy kitten had black spots on its belly.*)

predict: in science or reading, to use given information to decide what will happen

prefixes/suffixes: letters added to the beginning or end of a word to change its meaning (*reorganize, hopeless*)

preposition: a word that shows the relationship between a noun or pronoun and other words in a phrase or sentence (*We sat by the fire. She walked through the door.*)

probability: the likelihood that something will happen, often shown with numbers

pronoun: a word that is used in place of a noun (*She gave the present to them.*)

ratio: a comparison of two quantities, often shown as a fraction (*The ratio of boys to girls in the class is 2 to 1, or 2/1.*)

sequence: the order in which events happen or in which items can be placed in a pattern

subject: in a sentence, the word or words that tell who or what the sentence is about (*Uncle Robert baked the cake. Everyone at the party ate it.*)

summary: a restatement of important ideas from a selection in the writer's own words

symmetry: in math and science, two or more sides or faces of an object that are mirror images of one another

line of symmetry

synonyms: words with the same, or almost the same, meaning (*delicious* and *tasty, funny* and *comical*)

Venn diagram: two or more overlapping circles used to compare and contrast two or more things

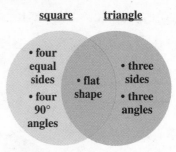

square   triangle

- four equal sides
- four 90° angles
- flat shape
- three sides
- three angles

verb: a word that describes an action or state of being (*He watched the fireworks.*)

writing prompt: on a test, a question or statement that you must respond to in writing

Practice Test and
Final Test Information

The remainder of this book is made up of two tests. On page 15, you will find a Practice Test. On page 43, you will find a Final Test. These tests will give you a chance to put the tips you have learned to work.

Here are some things to remember as you take these tests:

- Be sure you understand all the directions before you begin each test.

- Ask an adult questions about the directions if you do not understand them.

- Work as quickly as you can during each test. There are no time limits on the Practice Test, but you should try to make good use of your time. There are suggested time limits on the Final Test to give you practice managing your time.

- You will notice little GO and STOP signs at the bottom of the test pages. When you see a GO sign, continue on to the next page if you feel ready. The STOP sign means you are at the end of a section. When you see a STOP sign, take a break.

- When you change an answer, be sure to erase your first mark completely.

- You can guess at an answer or skip difficult items and go back to them later.

- Use the tips you have learned whenever you can.

- After you have completed your tests, check your answers with the answer key.

- It is OK to be a little nervous. You may even do better.

- When you complete all the lessons in this book, you will be on your way to test success!

Multiple Choice Questions

You have probably seen multiple choice questions before. They are the most common type of question used on standardized tests. To answer a multiple choice question, you must choose one answer from a number of choices.

EXAMPLE	**Another word for <u>unsafe</u> is _____.**

    Ⓐ safe

    Ⓑ dangerous

    Ⓒ unkind

    Ⓓ careful

Sometimes you will know the answer right away. Other times you won't. To answer multiple choice questions on a test, do the following:

- Read the directions carefully. If you're not sure what you're supposed to do, you might make a lot of mistakes.
- First answer any easy questions whose answers you are sure you know.
- When you come to a harder question, circle the question number. You can come back to this question after you have finished all the easier ones.
- When you're ready to answer a hard question, throw out answers that you know are wrong. You can do this by making an **X** after each choice you know is not correct. The last choice left is probably the correct one.

Testing It Out

Now look at the sample question more closely.

Think: I know that *safe* is the opposite of *unsafe*, so **A** cannot be the correct answer. I think that *cautious* is like being *careful*, so **D** is probably not the right answer.

Now I have to choose between **C** and **B**. Let's see: *unkind* has the word *kind* in it, and **un** usually means *not*, so I think that *unkind* means *not kind*. However, something that is *dangerous* is definitely not safe. So **B** must be the correct choice.

Fill-in-the-Blank Questions

On some tests, you will be given multiple choice questions where you must fill in something that's missing from a phrase, sentence, equation, or passage. These are called "fill-in-the-blank" questions.

EXAMPLE   **Tricia felt _____ that Robyn could not come to her party.**

    Ⓐ disturbed

    Ⓑ distorted

    Ⓒ dissolved

    Ⓓ disappointed

To answer fill-in-the-blank questions:

- First read the item with a blank that needs to be filled.
- See if you can think of the answer even before you look at your choices.
- Even if the answer you first thought of is one of the choices, be sure to check the other choices. There may be an even better answer.
- For harder questions, try to fit every answer choice into the blank. Underline clue words that may help you find the correct answer. Write an **X** after answers that do not fit. Choose the answer that does fit.

Testing It Out

Now look at the sample question above more closely.

Think: Choice **A** says, "Tricia felt *disturbed* that Robyn could not come to her party." I guess someone *might* feel disturbed if a friend could not come to her party.

Choice **B** says, "Tricia felt *dissolved* that Robyn could not come to her party." That sounds silly—people don't feel dissolved. That choice is wrong.

Choice **C** says, "Tricia felt *distorted* that Robyn could not come to her party." I have never heard of anyone feeling distorted. That choice must be wrong, too.

Choice **D** says, "Tricia felt *disappointed* that Robyn could not come to her party." This is how I would feel if a friend could not come to my party. I'll choose **D**.

True/False Questions

A true/false question asks you to read a statement and decide if it is right (true) or wrong (false). Sometimes you will be asked to write **T** for true or **F** for false. Most of the time you must fill in a bubble next to the correct answer.

> **EXAMPLE**   **Milk is the only ingredient in yogurt.**
>
>   Ⓐ true
>
>   Ⓑ false

To answer true/false questions on a test, think about the following:

* True/false sections contain more questions than other sections of a test. If there is a time limit on the test, you may need to go a little more quickly than usual. Do not spend too much time on any one question.
* First answer all of the easy questions. Circle the numbers next to harder ones and come back to them later.
* If you have time left after completing all the questions, quickly double-check your answers.
* True/false questions with words like *always, never, none, only,* and *every* are usually false. This is because they limit a statement so much.

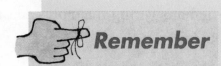

Remember

True/false questions with words like *always, never, none, only,* and *every* are usually false.

Testing It Out

Now look at the sample question more closely.

Think: I see the word *only* in this statement. I know that milk is the main ingredient in yogurt—it tastes a lot like milk. But some kinds of yogurt have fruit in them, and I think they must have sugar, too. I will mark this answer **B** for false.

Matching Questions

Matching questions ask you to find pairs of words or phrases that go together. The choices are often shown in columns.

EXAMPLE	Match items that mean the same, or almost the same, thing.

1 **happy**   Ⓐ mournful   1 Ⓐ Ⓑ Ⓒ Ⓓ

2 **angry**   Ⓑ flabbergasted   2 Ⓐ Ⓑ Ⓒ Ⓓ

3 **surprised** Ⓒ joyful   3 Ⓐ Ⓑ Ⓒ Ⓓ

4 **sad**   Ⓓ furious   4 Ⓐ Ⓑ Ⓒ Ⓓ

When answering matching questions on tests, there are some simple guidelines you can use:

• When you first look at a matching question, you will probably be able to spot some of the matches right away. So match the easiest choices first.

• If you come to a word you don't know, look for prefixes, suffixes, or root words to help figure out its meaning.

• Work down one column at a time. It is confusing to switch back and forth.

Testing It Out

Now look at the sample question more closely.

Think: What's a word from the second column that goes with *happy*? *Joyful* has the word *joy* in it, which is like happiness, so the answer to **1** must be **C.**

I know that *furious* is another word for *angry*, so the answer to 2 is **D.**

I'm not sure which of the remaining choices means the same as *surprised*, so I'll come back to that one.

For *sad*, I'm not sure what the best match is; however, I see that *mournful* has the word *mourn* in it, and people mourn when someone dies. Since people mourn when someone dies and they are also sad, then I'll choose **A** as the match for *sad*.

Going back to *surprised*, the only remaining choice is **B**, *flabbergasted*. That must be the correct choice, since I am fairly certain of my other answers.

Analogy Questions

Analogies are a special kind of question. In an analogy question, you are asked to figure out the relationship between two things. Then you must complete another pair with the same relationship.

EXAMPLE	**Carrot is to vegetable as orange is to _____.**

Ⓐ celery   Ⓒ apple

Ⓑ sweet   Ⓓ fruit

Analogies usually have two pairs of items. In the question above the two pairs are carrot/vegetable and orange/_____. To answer analogy questions on standardized tests, do the following:

- Find the missing item that completes the second pair. To do this, you must figure out how the first pair of items relate to each other. Try to form a sentence that explains how they are related.
- Next, use your sentence to figure out the missing word in the second pair of items.
- For more difficult analogies, try each answer choice in the sentence you formed. Choose the answer that fits best.

Testing It Out

Now look at the sample question more closely.

Think: How are carrots and vegetables related? A carrot is a kind of vegetable. So if I use the word *orange* in this sentence, I'd say, an *orange* is a kind of _____.

Choice **A** is *celery*. If I use *celery* to complete the sentence, I end up with *An orange is a kind of celery*. I think that celery is a vegetable. That choice must be wrong.

Choice **B** is *sweet*. *An orange is a kind of sweet*. No, that's not right, either. Oranges are sweet, but they're not a kind of sweet.

Choice **C** is *apple*. *An orange is a kind of apple*. I know that that answer is wrong because that sentence makes no sense.

Choice **D** would be *An orange is a kind of fruit*. Yes, I think that's true. So the answer must be **D**.

Short Answer Questions

Some test questions don't give you answers to choose from; instead, you must write short answers in your own words. These are called "short answer" or "open response" questions. For example:

 EXAMPLE

Which animal does not fit into the group?

_____

Why?

_____

When you must write short answers to questions on a standardized test:

* Make sure to respond directly to the question that is being asked.
* Your response should be short but complete. Don't waste time including unnecessary information. On the other hand, make sure to answer the entire question, not just a part of it.
* Write in complete sentences unless the directions say you don't have to.
* Double-check your answers for spelling, punctuation, and grammar mistakes.

Testing It Out
Now look at the sample question more closely.

 Think: Squirrels, rabbits, and skunks are all mammals. They have fur and four legs. But butterflies are insects. So *butterfly* must be the animal that does not fit.

Since there are no instructions about what to write for each answer, I should use complete sentences. So I'll write:

Which animal does not fit into the group?

The butterfly does not fit into the group.

Why?

A butterfly is an insect. All the other animals shown are mammals.

Name _____

Lesson 1   Story Reading

SAMPLE A

Suzie and Luis were up before their parents. They went outside the tent and looked at the sun coming up over the mountains.

Find the picture that shows where Suzie and Luis were.

at the beach   in the mountains   in the desert
Ⓐ   Ⓑ   Ⓒ

SAMPLE B

Find the words that best complete the sentence.

Orange juice _____ .

tastes good   from trees   for breakfast
Ⓕ   Ⓖ   Ⓗ

Look at each answer choice before marking the one you think is right.

Skip difficult items and come back to them later. Take your best guess when you don't know which answer is right.

For many people, morning is the best time of the day. The stories and poem you will read next will talk about some of the things that make mornings special.

GO

Name _____

Directions: This is a story about a family vacation. Read the story and then do numbers 1–7.

We're Not in Kansas Anymore

"I guess we're not in Kansas any more." Suzie smiled at her younger brother and walked toward the creek. Luis ran to catch up with her and took her hand. Both were wearing heavy sweaters to keep warm in the chilly morning air.

They sat down on a boulder beside the mountain stream. Across the stream was a meadow, and beyond that was a rocky base of a huge mountain. In fact, they were surrounded by mountains, many of which still had snow on them.

"Look, Suzie, cows." Luis pointed at several animals that had wandered into the meadow.

"I don't think they are cows, Buddy. They look like elk. I think they are almost like deer, but bigger."

Luis snuggled closer to his sister. He loved it when she called him "Buddy," and he was convinced she was the smartest person in the world, or at least the smartest kid.

GO

Test Prep

Name _____

The family had arrived the night before at the campground. Mr. and Mrs. Montoya had set the tent up while the kids were sleeping in the back of the car. They woke the children up and helped them into their sleeping bags, but neither Suzie nor Luis had taken a look around. This morning was their first chance to see where they had camped.

As the sun rose higher over the top of the mountain, fish started dimpling the surface of the pool below the boulder on which the children sat. Each time the fish rose to the surface, they left a small ring of water that spread across the pond. As the rings bumped into one another, they made glittering patterns in the sunlight.

"I wonder what the fish are doing?" wondered Suzie out loud.

"Probably eating breakfast," answered a voice. They turned to see their mother standing behind them.

Mrs. Montoya hugged the children, and the three of them watched the fish quietly for a few minutes.

"Let's head back to the tent." suggested Mrs. Montoya. "Maybe we can convince Dad to cook us some breakfast. We have a busy day ahead of us."

1 **The children in this story seem to**

   Ⓐ spend very little time together.

   Ⓑ enjoy visiting their relatives.

   Ⓒ love each other very much.

2 **Luis calls the elk cows because**

   Ⓕ he doesn't know what elk are.

   Ⓖ he is making a joke.

   Ⓗ they look like deer.

GO

3 **Which of these will the children probably do next?**

Ⓐ walk over to the elk

Ⓑ eat breakfast

Ⓒ set up the tents

4 **Find the sentence that best completes the story.**

Mr. Montoya is fixing breakfast. _____ . Then he will cook pancakes.

Ⓕ He is getting his fishing rod ready.

Ⓖ The tent is large enough for the family.

Ⓗ First he will make a fire.

5 **Find the word that best completes the sentence.**

Mount Wheeler is the _____ peak in New Mexico.

Ⓐ high   Ⓑ higher   Ⓒ highest

6 **The children wore sweaters in the chilly morning air. A word that means the** *opposite* **of chilly is**

Ⓕ warm   Ⓖ cool   Ⓗ damp

7 **The meadow was at the base of a rocky cliff. Find another word that means rocky.**

Ⓐ dirty   Ⓑ stony   Ⓒ swampy

GO

Name _____

Directions: This story is about a girl who spends each Saturday morning with her uncle. Read the story and then do numbers 8–12.

Skim the story then skim the questions.
Answer the easiest question first.

A Saturday Morning Surprise

Almost every Saturday morning, Uncle Bob stopped by Vanna's apartment to pick her up. Uncle Bob was her mother's older brother and had been her father's best friend. Vanna missed her father since he died a few years ago, but she was glad she had Uncle Bob.

On this Saturday morning, Uncle Bob said he had a surprise for Vanna. After saying good-bye to her mother, they took the elevator down to the street. Instead of getting in the car, she and Uncle Bob walked down the entrance to the subway and got on the next car that came by. They rode for about 15 minutes, then got off at a stop Vanna had never visited before. They walked up the stairs to the exit, and Vanna found herself in front of a building with huge columns holding up the roof.

"This is the Museum of Natural History, Vanna. It has some of the neatest

things you could imagine. I thought you might enjoy spending the day here."

Vanna was speechless as they walked up the steps and through the doors. There, in the middle of a huge hallway, was a dinosaur skeleton! She and Uncle Bob walked over to a museum guide who was telling the story of the dinosaur. Vanna hung on every word she said, and when the guide had finished, Vanna was able to ask some questions.

Uncle Bob then led her over to another room. It was warm and dark, but at the far end there was a glow of light. As they got closer, a recording said, "Welcome to the Living Volcano." This room was just like being inside a real volcano. Vanna loved science, and she was sure this was going to be one of the best mornings ever with Uncle Bob.

GO

Name _____

8 Look at the squares to the right. They show some of the things that might be found in a natural history museum. One of the squares is empty. Find the sentence that tells something else that might be found in a natural history museum.

   Ⓕ lightning display

   Ⓖ famous paintings

   Ⓗ old cars

   Ⓙ live animals

9 The story says that "Vanna was speechless." What does that probably mean?

   Ⓐ She was disappointed at the surprise.

   Ⓑ Uncle Bob didn't give her a chance to talk.

   Ⓒ She was so excited she didn't know what to say.

   Ⓓ The museum guide did all the talking.

GO

10 **Vanna did some research about museums. Find the best topic sentence for her paragraph.**

_____. *Art museums and science museums are the most well-known. Museums have also been built for trains, cars, and even toys.*

Ⓕ Some museums are free.

Ⓖ Students often take trips to museums.

Ⓗ Art museums have many paintings.

Ⓙ There are several kinds of museums.

11 **In the story, the roof of the museum is held up by <u>columns</u>. The <u>columns</u> probably look like**

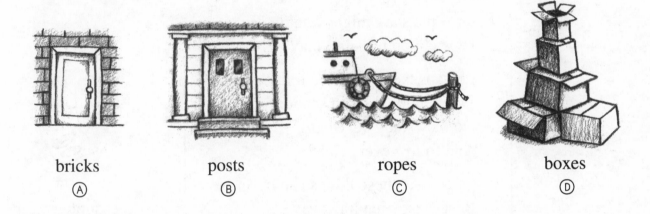

bricks	posts	ropes	boxes
Ⓐ	Ⓑ	Ⓒ	Ⓓ

12 **Find the sentence that is complete and correctly written.**

Ⓕ Crowded subway in the morning.

Ⓖ Museum opening at nine o'clock

Ⓗ They had breakfast before leaving.

Ⓙ Vanna getting ready early.

STOP

Name _____

Lesson 2 Poem Reading

SAMPLE
A

Every Monday, as we know,
Up we get, and off we go.

The writer is probably talking about going off to

Ⓐ school   Ⓑ dinner   Ⓒ shopping

Directions: Ben wrote this poem about something that couldn't happen. Read the
poem and then do numbers 1–7.

What Do You Think?

I wonder if the sun gets tired
Of rising every day?
Or if the stars might want to see
How children like to play?

Perhaps the moon would like to learn
What children do in school?
Do they study very hard
And follow every rule?

Of course, these things can never be
Because it's nature's way,
For moon and stars to toil at night,
And sun to work all day.

The right answer is
not always stated
exactly in the poem.

1 **This poem is mostly about**

Ⓐ the moon and stars changing
   places with the sun.

Ⓑ children studying in school.

Ⓒ children pretending they are the
   sun, moon, or stars.

2 **This poem wonders if**

Ⓕ the moon is bored.

Ⓖ the stars are funny.

Ⓗ the sun is tired.

GO

Name _____

3 In this poem, "nature's way" means

(A) the way things are now.

(B) the way things should be.

(C) the way things were before.

4 Choose the words that best complete this sentence.

The moon _____.

(F) shining at night

(G) is bright tonight

(H) in the dark sky

5 The moon and stars toil in the poem. Another word for toil is

(A) play.

(B) travel.

(C) work.

6 Find the word that can take the place of Millie and Larry in the sentence below.

Millie and Larry went for a run this morning.

(F) They

(G) Them

(H) It

7 Find the picture that shows what the moon is doing in the poem.

(A)　　　　　　　(B)　　　　　　　(C)

GO

Name _____

Directions: Ben started this poem. Help him finish it by choosing the right words to fill the blanks.

A cow is such a silly thing,
It makes a silly sound, _____(8)_____
It lives on a _____(9)_____
Inside a barn
And gives us milk, _____(10)_____.

Directions: For numbers 11 and 12, find the answer that best fills each blank.

A _____(11)_____ *is such a pretty thing,*
with eyes and coat of brown.
It lives in the _____(12)_____
And hides among trees
But rarely makes a sound.

8 Ⓕ bark

Ⓖ meow

Ⓗ oink

Ⓙ moo

9 Ⓐ beach

Ⓑ farm

Ⓒ street

Ⓓ porch

10 Ⓕ too

Ⓖ also

Ⓗ yum

Ⓙ wow

11 Ⓐ (food name)

Ⓑ (person name)

Ⓒ (animal name)

Ⓓ (time name)

12 Ⓕ (place name)

Ⓖ (animal name)

Ⓗ (food name)

Ⓙ (time name)

13 **Which idea is not part of these poems?**

Ⓐ animal names

Ⓑ where animals live

Ⓒ animal sounds

Ⓓ what animals eat

STOP

Name _____

Lesson 3 Writing

Directions: Read the paragraph about one student's favorite class. Then write one or two sentences to answer each question below.

> My favorite class is art. I like to draw, and I like to paint. The teacher is very nice. He shows us how to do new things. I always look forward to this class. It would be even better if it were longer.

What is your favorite class?

_____

_____

_____

_____

Why is it your favorite?

_____

_____

_____

_____

What might make this class even better?

_____

_____

_____

_____

GO

Name _____

Directions: Read the short story about a friend's visit. Then think about a fiction story that you would like to write. Write one or two sentences to answer each question below.

Juan looked at the clock. He paced across the floor. His best friend, Bill, was coming to visit for the first time in six months. Bill had moved very far away. Juan wondered if they would still feel like good friends.

The doorbell rang, and Juan raced to answer it. Bill looked a bit unsure. Juan smiled and started talking just as he always had when they had lived near one another. He made Bill feel comfortable. As the day went on, it felt like old times.

Think about the main character. Who is it? What is he or she like?

_____

_____

_____

Where does the story take place? When does the story take place? Now? In the past? In the future?

_____

_____

_____

What problem will the main character have? How will he or she try to solve the problem?

_____

_____

_____

STOP

Name _____

Lesson 1 Word Analysis

Find the word in which the underlined letters have the same sound as the picture name.

br<u></u>ead   bl<u></u>ack   b<u></u>owl

(A)   (B)   (C)

Repeat the directions to yourself as you look at the answer choices. Think carefully about what you should do.

Directions: For numbers 1–4, choose the best answer.

1 **Find the word that has the same beginning sound as**

 .

  (A) f<u></u>rame.

  (B) f<u></u>lame.

  (C) f<u></u>ork.

2 **Find the word that has the same ending sound as**

 .

  (F) mea<u>nt</u>.

  (G) sta<u>nd</u>.

  (H) ear<u>n</u>.

3 **Look at the first word. Find the other word that has the same vowel sound as the underlined part.**

fl<u>oa</u>t

  (A) block

  (B) board

  (C) chose

  (D) pool

4 **Look at the underlined word. Find a word that can be added to the underlined word to make a compound word.**

<u>door</u>

  (F) knock   (H) window

  (G) open   (J) step

STOP

Name _____

Lesson 2   Vocabulary

Directions: For Samples A and B and numbers 1 and 2, find the answer that means the same or about the same as the underlined word.

SAMPLE A   consider this idea

ⓐ ignore   © agree with

ⓑ think about   Ⓓ like

SAMPLE B   raise a flag

Ⓕ lift   Ⓖ lower

Ⓗ fly   Ⓙ hold

---

1   liberty for everyone

ⓐ freedom   © work

ⓑ vacation   Ⓓ food

2   long journey

Ⓕ story   Ⓗ road

Ⓖ movie   Ⓙ trip

Directions: For number 3, find the word that means the opposite of the underlined word.

3   thrilling ride

ⓐ long

ⓑ exciting

© boring

Ⓓ interesting

Think about where you heard or read the underlined word before. Try each answer in the blank.

Directions: For numbers 4 and 5, read the sentence with the missing word and then read the question. Find the best answer to the question.

4   The weather will _____ tomorrow.

Which word means the weather will get better?

Ⓕ improve   Ⓗ worsen

Ⓖ change   Ⓙ vary

5   The _____ followed the rabbit into the forest.

Which word means a dog followed the rabbit into the forest?

ⓐ traveler   © hound

ⓑ hunter   Ⓓ hawk

GO

Name _____

Directions: For Sample C and numbers 6 and 7, read the sentences. Then choose the word that correctly completes both sentences.

SAMPLE
C

The _____ swam in the pond.

You have to _____ your head here.

Ⓐ fish   Ⓑ duck   Ⓒ children   Ⓓ lower

6   Who will _____ this problem?

The _____ on the shovel is broken.

Ⓐ solve   Ⓑ blade   Ⓒ cause   Ⓓ handle

7   Can I take your _____?

She will _____ him to do it.

Ⓕ order   Ⓖ tell   Ⓗ coat   Ⓙ hat

Use the meaning of the sentence to find the answer.

Directions: For numbers 8 and 9, read the story. For each blank, look at the words with the same number. Find the word from each list that fits best in the blank.

Dogs need __(8)__ to stay healthy. They should be given

an __(9)__ to play for at least 15 minutes each day.

8   Ⓐ exercise   Ⓑ leashes   Ⓒ treats   Ⓓ dishes

9   Ⓕ examination   Ⓖ assistance   Ⓗ individual   Ⓙ opportunity

STOP

Name _____

Lesson 3 Language Mechanics

Directions: For Sample A and numbers 1 and 2, find the punctuation mark that is needed in the sentence.

SAMPLE A	The television is too loud			
	?	.	,	None
	Ⓐ	Ⓑ	Ⓒ	Ⓓ

1 How many fish did you catch

   ?   .   ,   None

  Ⓐ   Ⓑ   Ⓒ   Ⓓ

2 Quick, let's get out of the rain

   ?   .   !   None

  Ⓕ   Ⓖ   Ⓗ   Ⓙ

Look for a mistake in capitalization or a missing punctuation mark in this part of the lesson.

Directions: For Sample B and numbers 3 and 4, which part needs a capital letter? If no capital letter is needed, mark "None."

SAMPLE B	My cousin	has a bird	named fluffy.	None
	Ⓐ	Ⓑ	Ⓒ	Ⓓ

3 Give this | piece of pie | to connie. | None

   Ⓐ   Ⓑ   Ⓒ   Ⓓ

4 Imo's class | will go to | Orlando, Florida. | None

   Ⓕ   Ⓖ   Ⓗ   Ⓙ

GO

Name _____

Directions: Find the sentence that has the correct capitalization and punctuation.

5 Ⓐ Our picnic is tomorrow!

Ⓑ Mr. ames will cook.

Ⓒ we'll meet Jenny there.

Ⓓ Sam and I will be there.

6 Ⓕ Who is playing.

Ⓖ The park is this way!

Ⓗ Call Jeff. He wants to come with us.

Ⓙ The game starts soon. let's hurry

Remember, in this part of the lesson you should find the answer with correct capitalization and punctuation.

SAMPLE C

Find the answer choice that shows the correct capitalization and punctuation for the underlined part.

Did you finish your project. Mine is almost done.

Ⓐ Project mine.

Ⓑ project? Mine

Ⓒ Project. Mine

Ⓓ Correct as it is

Directions: For numbers 7 and 8, look at the underlined part of the sentence. Choose the answer that shows the best capitalization and punctuation for that part.

(7)   None of Winnies friends told her about the surprise

(8) birthday party. She was the captain of the softball team. The other players wanted to do something special for her.

7 Ⓐ Winnies friend's

Ⓑ Winnies' friends

Ⓒ Winnie's friends

Ⓓ Correct as it is

8 Ⓕ team! The

Ⓖ team the

Ⓗ team, the

Ⓙ Correct as it is

STOP

Name _____

Lesson 4 Spelling

Directions: Find the word that is spelled correctly and best fits in the blank.

1 **We picked _____ in our garden.**

Ⓐ berries   Ⓒ berrys

Ⓑ berrese   Ⓓ berreis

2 **The _____ helped me.**

Ⓕ nourse   Ⓗ nurce

Ⓖ nirse   Ⓙ nurse

3 **The answer to this problem is a _____ .**

Ⓐ frackshun   Ⓒ fracteon

Ⓑ fraction   Ⓓ fracton

4 **Did you _____ the page?**

Ⓕ tare   Ⓗ tair

Ⓖ tear   Ⓙ taer

5 **This _____ was in the school paper.**

Ⓐ artical   Ⓒ article

Ⓑ articel   Ⓓ articol

Directions: For Sample A and numbers 6–8, find the underlined word that is not spelled correctly.

SAMPLE A

Ⓐ <u>identify</u> a bird

Ⓑ <u>bottle</u> of juice

Ⓒ <u>quiet</u> room

Ⓓ All correct

6 Ⓐ easy <u>lesson</u>

Ⓑ last <u>forevr</u>

Ⓒ <u>paddle</u> a canoe

Ⓓ All correct

7 Ⓕ good <u>balance</u>

Ⓖ delicious <u>stew</u>

Ⓗ <u>private</u> property

Ⓙ All correct

8 Ⓐ great <u>relief</u>

Ⓑ our <u>mayor</u>

Ⓒ <u>sunnie</u> day

Ⓓ All correct

If an item is too difficult, skip it and come back to it later.

STOP

Name _____

Lesson 5 Computation

Directions: For Samples A and B and numbers 1–4, find the answer that is the solution to the problem. If the answer is not given, choose "None of these."

SAMPLE A

$$\begin{array}{r} 23 \\ + 16 \\ \hline \end{array}$$

Ⓐ 17

Ⓑ 29

Ⓒ 39

Ⓓ 84

Ⓔ None of these

SAMPLE B

$$\begin{array}{r} 48 \\ - 43 \\ \hline \end{array}$$

Ⓕ 10

Ⓖ 25

Ⓗ 41

Ⓙ 91

Ⓚ None of these

Pay attention to the operation sign so you know what to do.
Be sure to transfer numbers correctly to scratch paper.

1

$115 + 71 =$

Ⓐ 44

Ⓑ 76

Ⓒ 176

Ⓓ 186

Ⓔ None of these

3

$$\begin{array}{r} \$9.38 \\ - 4.51 \\ \hline \end{array}$$

Ⓐ $4.87

Ⓑ $5.87

Ⓒ $5.32

Ⓓ $13.89

Ⓔ None of these

2

$$\begin{array}{r} 52 \\ 16 \\ + 5 \\ \hline \end{array}$$

Ⓕ 21

Ⓖ 57

Ⓗ 63

Ⓙ 83

Ⓚ None of these

4

$5 \times 5 =$

Ⓕ 10

Ⓖ 25

Ⓗ 35

Ⓙ 55

Ⓚ None of these

STOP

Name _____

Lesson 1 | Mathematics Skills

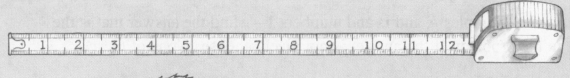

 How many inches long is the fish?

ⓐ 5 inches

ⓑ 6 inches

ⓒ 8 inches

ⓓ 12 inches

Read the problem carefully. Look for key words, numbers, and figures. Look carefully at all the answer choices.

If you use scratch paper, transfer the numbers correctly. Work neatly and carefully so you don't make a careless mistake.

GO

Name _____

1 What is the best estimate of the number of beans on the plate?

Ⓐ 30

Ⓑ 20

Ⓒ 12

Ⓓ 10

2 Look at the number pattern in the box. Find the number that is missing.

11, 22, _____, 44, 55

Ⓕ 33

Ⓖ 23

Ⓗ 32

Ⓙ 42

3 Look at the clock. How long will it take the minute hand to reach the 6?

Ⓐ 3 minutes

Ⓑ 5 minutes

Ⓒ 12 minutes

Ⓓ 15 minutes

4 Marlow noticed that the parking lot at the store had 11 red cars, 6 blue cars, 4 white cars, and 3 cars of other colors. If someone leaves the building and walks to a car, which color car is it most likely to be?

Ⓕ red

Ⓖ blue

Ⓗ white

Ⓙ another color

5 Sandy had 5 .

She read 2 .

Find the number sentence that tells how many books Sandy has left to read.

Ⓐ $5 + 2 = 7$

Ⓑ $5 - 2 = 3$

Ⓒ $2 + 3 = 5$

Ⓓ $2 - 1 = 1$

GO

Name _____

6 Look at the pattern of fruit. Which of these is the missing piece of fruit?

- Ⓕ orange
- Ⓗ pear
- Ⓖ banana
- Ⓙ apple

7 Mr. Lowell paid $0.59 for a bag of chips and $0.39 for a bottle of juice. How much money did he spend all together?

- Ⓐ $0.79
- Ⓑ $0.88
- Ⓒ $0.89
- Ⓓ $0.98

8 Look at the number sentences. Find the number that goes in the boxes to make both number sentences true.

$6 + \square = 7$
$7 - \square = 6$

- Ⓕ 1
- Ⓖ 0
- Ⓗ 13
- Ⓙ 7

9 Look at the picture. What number tells how many blocks are in the picture?

- Ⓐ 100
- Ⓑ 115
- Ⓒ 110
- Ⓓ 15

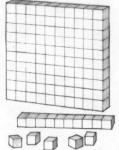

Directions: For numbers 10 and 11, estimate the answer to each problem. You do not have to find an exact answer.

10 Which two things together would cost about $30.00?

- Ⓕ hat and shirt
- Ⓖ belt and socks
- Ⓗ shirt and socks
- Ⓙ hat and belt

$18.00
$25.00
$9.00
$13.00

11 Use estimation to find which of these is closest to 1000.

- Ⓐ 591 + 573
- Ⓒ 392 + 589
- Ⓑ 499 + 409
- Ⓓ 913 + 183

GO

Name _____

Directions: The third grade students at Millbrook School made a graph about where they wanted to go on vacation. Study the graph, then do numbers 12–14.

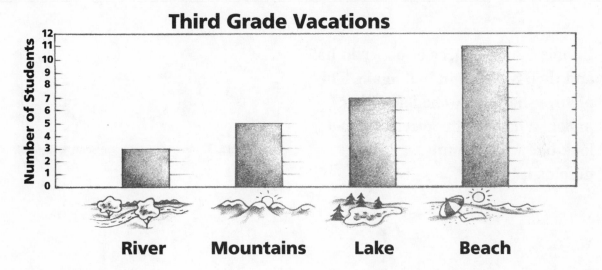

12 Which of these is another way to show how many students went to the beach?

Ⓕ THL THL I

Ⓖ THL I

Ⓗ THL THL

Ⓙ THL THL IIII

13 How many students went to a lake for vacation?

Ⓐ 11   Ⓒ 8

Ⓑ 7   Ⓓ 5

14 Two of the students changed their minds and decided to go to a lake instead of the beach. How many students then wanted to go to a lake?

Ⓕ 7   Ⓗ 5

Ⓖ 8   Ⓙ 9

GO

Name _____

15 Look at the paper clip and the pencils. Which pencil is about three inches longer than the paper clip?

Ⓐ   Ⓑ   Ⓒ   Ⓓ

16 Bonnie folded a piece of paper in half and then folded it in half again. The picture shows how she folded her paper. What will the piece of paper look like when Bonnie unfolds it?

Ⓕ   Ⓖ   Ⓗ   Ⓙ

17 Find the answer that shows 35 peanuts.

Ⓐ   Ⓑ

Ⓒ   Ⓓ

STOP

Name _____

Lesson 1

Directions: Study the time line that shows when four U. S. Presidents took office. Then do numbers 1–3.

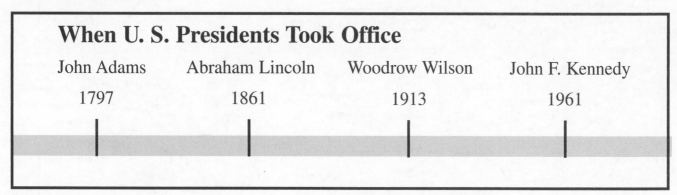

When U. S. Presidents Took Office

John Adams	Abraham Lincoln	Woodrow Wilson	John F. Kennedy
1797	1861	1913	1961

1 **Which person on the time line became President first?**

Ⓐ Woodrow Wilson

Ⓑ John Adams

Ⓒ John F. Kennedy

Ⓓ Abraham Lincoln

2 **Which person on the time line became President last?**

Ⓕ John F. Kennedy

Ⓖ Woodrow Wilson

Ⓗ Abraham Lincoln

Ⓙ John Adams

3 **Which person on the time line became President in 1861?**

Ⓐ John Adams

Ⓑ John F. Kennedy

Ⓒ Woodrow Wilson

Ⓓ Abraham Lincoln

GO

Name _____

Directions: Study the map of the United States. Then do numbers 4–7.

4 **Which state is a peninsula?**

Ⓕ Nevada

Ⓖ Florida

Ⓗ Washington

Ⓙ Georgia

6 **Which state is on the West Coast?**

Ⓕ California

Ⓖ North Carolina

Ⓗ Utah

Ⓙ Minnesota

5 **Which state is farthest north?**

Ⓐ Texas

Ⓑ Arizona

Ⓒ New York

Ⓓ Kansas

7 **Which state is east of Nebraska?**

Ⓐ Oregon

Ⓑ Mississippi

Ⓒ Idaho

Ⓓ New Mexico

STOP

Name _____

Science

Lesson 1

Directions: Read the Venn diagram, and then do numbers 1–4.

African Elephant
- ears cover shoulder
- back dips
- two finger-like lobes at the end of trunk
- smooth forehead
- wrinkled skin

Both Elephants
- long tusks
- tail
- eat plants

Indian Elephants
- ears do not cover shoulder
- back arches
- one lobe on trunk
- two lumps on forehead
- less wrinkled skin

1 **Which elephants have long tusks?**

Ⓐ Only the African elephants

Ⓑ Only the Indian elephants

Ⓒ Both the African and Indian elephants

2 **Which elephants have one lobe at the end of their trunks?**

Ⓕ Only the African elephants

Ⓖ Only the Indian elephants

Ⓗ Both the African and Indian elephants

3 **Which elephants have ears that cover their shoulders?**

Ⓐ Only the African elephants

Ⓑ Only the Indian elephants

Ⓒ Both the African and Indian elephants

4 **Which elephants eat plants?**

Ⓕ Only the African elephants

Ⓖ Only the Indian elephants

Ⓗ Both the African and Indian elephants

GO

Name _____

Directions: For numbers 5–7, find each true statement.

5 Ⓐ Chlorophyll is the process in which plants turn water and air into food.

   Ⓑ Photosynthesis is the process in which plants turn light, water, and air into food.

   Ⓒ Plants need leaves in order to turn water and air into food.

   Ⓓ Light is not necessary for plants to turn water and air into food.

6 Ⓕ The seeds take in light and nutrients from the air.

   Ⓖ The leaves take in water and nutrients from the soil.

   Ⓗ The roots take in water and nutrients from the soil.

   Ⓙ The flowers take in light and water from the soil.

7 Ⓐ Conifers (example: pine trees) lose their leaves in the fall.

   Ⓑ Conifers stay green year round.

   Ⓒ Conifers have broad leaves.

   Ⓓ Conifers' leaves turn gold in the fall.

Directions: Do numbers 8–11.

8 **Which is not part of a flower?**

   Ⓕ pistil

   Ⓖ stamen

   Ⓗ thorax

   Ⓙ petal

9 **Which part of the flower holds the pollen?**

   Ⓐ stamen

   Ⓑ pistil

   Ⓒ sepal

   Ⓓ petal

10 **Food-making material in leaves is called**

   Ⓕ chlorophyll.

   Ⓖ photosynthesis.

   Ⓗ sunlight.

   Ⓙ water.

11 **Which does a plant not need to grow?**

   Ⓐ light   Ⓒ soil

   Ⓑ water   Ⓓ sand

STOP

Name _____

0:25
Pages 43–46
Time Limit:
approx. 25 minutes

Reading and Language Arts

SAMPLE A

Find the underlined part of the sentence that is the <u>simple subject</u>.

Two <u>planes</u> flew <u>over</u> our <u>house</u> yesterday <u>morning</u>.

     Ⓐ   Ⓑ   Ⓒ   Ⓓ

Directions: Read this story about a woman pilot and then do numbers 1–7.

THE FORGOTTEN FLYER

More than 80 years ago, Jacqueline Cochran was born to a poor family in Pensacola, Florida. Like many girls at the time, she went to work at an early age. When she was just eight years old, Jacqueline Cochran worked in a cotton mill. Jacqueline went on to do many things in her life, but her great dream was to become an aviator.

When Ms. Cochran became a pilot in the 1930s, flying was still in its infancy. Planes were still new inventions, and only the most daring men flew them. Almost no women were flyers, but that didn't stop Jacqueline. She took flying lessons, and was soon good enough to enter famous races. In 1938, she won first prize in a contest to fly across America.

Near the beginning of World War II, Jacqueline trained women in England to become pilots. She later did the same thing for over a thousand American women. In 1945, she was awarded the Distinguished Service Medal, one of America's highest honors.

When the roar of jet planes replaced the clatter of propeller planes, Jacqueline learned to fly them, and soon was the first woman to fly faster than the speed of sound. Jacqueline also set many other records, including flying higher than anyone had before her.

In many ways, Jacqueline Cochran is the forgotten flyer. But she should be remembered, because this aviation pioneer helped establish flying as one of our most important means of transportation.

GO

Name _____

1 **What makes Jacqueline Cochran so special?**

Ⓐ working at an early age

Ⓑ founding a business

Ⓒ being an early flyer

Ⓓ being born in Florida

2 **This story suggests that**

Ⓕ jets came after propeller planes.

Ⓖ propeller planes came after jets.

Ⓗ many people flew in the 1930s.

Ⓙ Jacqueline Cochran founded an airline.

3 **Another way to say "flying faster than the speed of sound" is**

Ⓐ making a loud sound.

Ⓑ breaking the sound barrier.

Ⓒ flying a loud plane.

Ⓓ winning an important race.

4 **Look at the picture of Jacqueline Cochran below. The picture shows Jacqueline**

Ⓕ winning an important award.

Ⓖ working at a mill.

Ⓗ with her invention.

Ⓙ getting ready to fly.

GO

Test Prep

Name _____

5 **The story says that "flying was still in its infancy" when Jacqueline began. What does this probably mean?**

Ⓐ It was something new.

Ⓑ She was very young.

Ⓒ Infants could fly.

Ⓓ Planes were small.

6 **Cotton is a kind of fabric.**

Find another thing that is a fabric.

Ⓕ paper   Ⓗ silk

Ⓖ a comb   Ⓙ shoes

7 *Roar* **is a word that sounds like the sound it names. Some other examples are** *buzz,* *splash,* **and** *croak.*

Find another word that sounds like the sound it names.

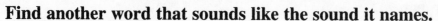

Ⓐ catch

Ⓑ beep

Ⓒ drive

Ⓓ loud

GO

Name _____

Directions: For numbers 8 and 9, find the word or words that best complete the sentence.

8 **My sister _____ to Space Camp.**

 Ⓕ gone   Ⓗ go

 Ⓖ going   Ⓙ went

9 **She said it was the _____ she had ever had.**

 Ⓐ funniest   Ⓒ most fun

 Ⓑ more fun   Ⓓ most funner

10 **Find the word that fits both sentences below.**

 We _____ at eight o'clock for the lake.
 The house on the _____ is mine.

 Ⓕ left   Ⓗ side

 Ⓖ went   Ⓙ right

11 **Find the underlined part of the sentence that is the simple subject.**

 A large tree grew beside the lake.
  Ⓐ   Ⓑ   Ⓒ   Ⓓ

STOP

Test Prep

Name _____

Directions: Read the passage. Then, answer numbers 12–21.

0:20
Pages 47–49
Time Limit:
approx. 20 minutes

Therapy Dogs

Therapy dogs can help patients **recover** from many illnesses. The dogs' owners or handlers bring them into hospital rooms and encourage patients to **interact** with the animals. Dogs sometimes get right up on patients' beds. People who are sick or recovering from surgery pet the dogs, brush them, talk to them, and even allow the friendly pets to **nuzzle** their faces. Studies have shown that interacting with dogs and other animals is highly **therapeutic**: it can **reduce** stress, lower blood pressure, and even promote healing.

Obviously, not all dogs are **well-suited** for this important job. To be a therapy dog, a dog must have a calm, friendly **disposition**. Some therapy dog owners feel their pets were born to help sick people get well.

12 **What is this passage mainly about?**

Ⓕ working dogs

Ⓖ therapy dogs

Ⓗ hospital volunteers

Ⓙ friendly pets

13 **Which words help you figure out the meaning of** *therapeutic*?

Ⓐ "well-suited for this important job"

Ⓑ "interacting with dogs and other animals"

Ⓒ "reduce stress, lower blood pressure"

Ⓓ "Studies have shown"

GO

Name _____

14 **Which word is a synonym for *recover*?**

    Ⓕ heal   Ⓗ suffer

    Ⓖ sleep   Ⓙ avoid

15 *Nuzzling* **is like**

    Ⓐ rubbing.   Ⓒ drinking.

    Ⓑ kissing.   Ⓓ biting.

16 **Which word is not a synonym for *reduce*?**

    Ⓕ shrink   Ⓗ increase

    Ⓖ lessen   Ⓙ decrease

17 **When you *interact* with another person, you**

    Ⓐ communicate with him or her.

    Ⓑ copy his or her behavior.

    Ⓒ avoid speaking to him or her.

    Ⓓ tell others about him or her.

18 **A person who is *well-suited* for a certain job is**

    Ⓕ wearing a special uniform.

    Ⓑ able to afford the right clothes for the job.

    Ⓗ someone who can do the job well.

    Ⓙ calm and gentle.

GO

19 *Disposition* **means about the same as**

Ⓐ breed.   Ⓒ work experience.

Ⓑ personality.   Ⓓ reputation.

20 **The writer of the passage mainly wants to**

Ⓕ persuade readers to volunteer in hospitals.

Ⓖ entertain readers with some dog stories.

Ⓗ give information about therapy dogs.

Ⓙ give information about one special dog.

21 **What kind of dog would probably not make a good therapy dog?**

Ⓐ a golden retriever   Ⓒ a dog that lived with children

Ⓑ an older dog   Ⓓ a dog that does not like to be petted

Directions: For numbers 22–25, decide whether each statement is true or false.

22 **Therapy dogs are pets that belong to patients.**

Ⓐ true   Ⓑ false

23 **The writer thinks that bringing therapy dogs into hospitals is a good idea.**

Ⓐ true   Ⓑ false

24 **No sick person would turn down a visit from a friendly dog.**

Ⓐ true   Ⓑ false

25 **Interacting with dogs probably makes some patients feel happier and calmer.**

Ⓐ true   Ⓑ false

STOP

Name _____

Directions: Read the passage. Then, answer numbers 26–34.

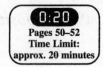

0:20
Pages 50–52
Time Limit:
approx. 20 minutes

MAKING CLAY MOVE

Beginning in the late 1900s, **claymation** became very popular. **Animators** have used clay animation to make several famous movies and TV commercials. However, claymation is not a new **technique**. In 1897 a clay-like **substance** called plasticine was invented. Moviemakers used plasticine to create clay animation films as early as 1908.

Here's how claymation works. First, an artist makes one or more clay models. Moviemakers **pose** each model, take a camera shot, and stop. Next they move the model a tiny bit (into a very slightly different pose), and **shoot** again. They continue to shoot, move the model, shoot, move the model, and so on. It takes many separate shots to make one second of film.

Today's animators usually use clays such as Sculpey™ or Fimo™. Computer techniques have made the claymation process much less **time-consuming**. However, the basics of clay animation have not changed in almost 100 years!

26 **What is this passage mainly about?**

Ⓕ plasticine

Ⓖ types of clay

Ⓗ claymation techniques and history

Ⓙ famous movies made with claymation

27 **An *animator* is someone who**

Ⓐ creates clay sculptures.

Ⓑ makes animated films.

Ⓒ uses claymation only.

Ⓓ invents clay substances.

28 **The word *claymation* comes from the words *clay* and**

Ⓕ movement.

Ⓖ technician.

Ⓗ concentration.

Ⓙ animation.

29 **Which word means the same as *technique*?**

Ⓐ technical

Ⓑ method

Ⓒ movie

Ⓓ talent

GO

Name _____

30 **Which word is a synonym for** *substance*?

  Ⓕ sound

  Ⓖ substitute

  Ⓗ liquid

  Ⓙ material

31 **What does it mean to** *pose* **something?**

  Ⓐ roll it into a ball

  Ⓑ squash it flat

  Ⓒ use it to make a model

  Ⓓ move it into a certain position

32 **In this passage, the word** *shoot* **means**

  Ⓕ to fire a gun.

  Ⓖ a part of a plant that has just begun to grow.

  Ⓗ to take a photograph or make a movie.

  Ⓙ to move quickly.

33 **Which word means the opposite of** *time-consuming*?

  Ⓐ speedy

  Ⓑ sluggish

  Ⓒ frustrating

  Ⓓ satisfying

34 **The writer of the passage mainly wants to**

  Ⓕ persuade readers to rent certain videotapes.

  Ⓖ entertain readers with some filmmaking stories.

  Ⓗ give information about claymation.

  Ⓙ give information about plasticine.

GO

Name _____

Directions: Choose the correct answer to each question to complete the analogies.

35 Rose is to flower as oak is to _____.

ⓐ leaf   ⓒ bush

ⓑ furniture   ⓓ tree

36 Begin is to cease as confuse is to _____.

ⓕ clarify   ⓗ continue

ⓖ annoy   ⓙ stop

37 Supermarket is to groceries as bookstore is to _____.

ⓐ food   ⓒ reading materials

ⓑ paper   ⓓ library

38 Fork is to eat as ruler is to _____.

ⓕ cut   ⓗ spoon

ⓖ measure   ⓙ inch

Directions: Match words with the same meanings. Mark the letter of your choice.

39 frothy   A delicious   **39** ⓐ ⓑ ⓒ ⓓ

40 tasty   B raw   **40** ⓐ ⓑ ⓒ ⓓ

41 uncooked   C foamy   **41** ⓐ ⓑ ⓒ ⓓ

42 spicy   D hot   **42** ⓐ ⓑ ⓒ ⓓ

Directions: Match words with opposite meanings. Mark the letter of your choice.

43 polite   F backward   **43** ⓕ ⓖ ⓗ ⓙ

44 behind   G rude   **44** ⓕ ⓖ ⓗ ⓙ

45 forward   H fantastic   **45** ⓕ ⓖ ⓗ ⓙ

46 realistic   J ahead   **46** ⓕ ⓖ ⓗ ⓙ

STOP

Name _____

Directions: Read the paragraph that tells how to make a peanut butter and jelly sandwich. Then think of something you like to make or do. Write a paragraph that tells how to make it. Use the words *first, next, then, last.*

These steps tell how to make a peanut butter and jelly sandwich. First get two pieces of bread, peanut butter, jelly, and a knife. Next spread peanut butter on one piece of bread. Then spread jelly on the other piece. Last press the two pieces of bread together.

0:20
Pages 53–54
Time Limit:
approx. 20 minutes

_____

_____

_____

_____

_____

_____

_____

_____

_____

_____

_____

_____

_____

_____

_____

_____

_____

GO

Name _____

Directions: Read the letter below. In the letter, a girl explains to her father why she should be allowed to try inline skating. Then think of something you would like to be allowed to do. Write a letter to explain to someone why you should be allowed to do it.

Dear Dad,

I would like to try inline skating. I know that you think it is not safe, but I would be very careful. I would follow every safety rule. I would wear a helmet, elbow pads, and knee pads. I would only skate in safe places. Please give me a chance.

Love,

Bonita

_____

_____

_____

_____

_____

_____

_____

_____

_____

_____

_____

_____

STOP

Pages 55–58
Time Limit:
approx. 20 minutes

Name _____

Basic Skills

SAMPLE A

Find the word in which the underlined letters have the same sound as the picture name.

Ⓐ last Ⓑ sleep Ⓒ clip Ⓓ ship

---

1   Ⓐ chase Ⓑ crisp Ⓒ club Ⓓ shirt

2 Find the word that has the same ending sound as

Ⓕ hand Ⓖ jump Ⓗ chance Ⓙ charm

3 Look at the first word. Find the other word that has the same vowel sound as the underlined part.

brought Ⓐ lost Ⓑ pound Ⓒ stone Ⓓ crowd

4 Look at the underlined word. Find a word that can be added to the underlined word to make a compound word.

air Ⓕ cut Ⓖ plane Ⓗ grass Ⓙ green

5 Find the word in which just the prefix is underlined.

Ⓐ preview Ⓑ decide Ⓒ alert Ⓓ monster

6 Find the word in which only the root word is underlined.

Ⓕ older Ⓖ cart Ⓗ roomy Ⓙ fully

7 Find the word in which only the suffix is underlined.

Ⓐ bundle Ⓑ mostly Ⓒ runner Ⓓ jumping

GO

Name _____

Directions: For Sample B and numbers 8 and 9, find the answer that means the same or about the same as the underlined word.

 extremely windy

    Ⓐ slightly   Ⓒ often

    Ⓑ somewhat Ⓓ very

8 famous **legend**

    Ⓐ person   Ⓒ place

    Ⓑ tale   Ⓓ painting

9 **create** a statue

    Ⓕ enjoy   Ⓗ see

    Ⓖ make   Ⓙ drop

Directions: Find the word that correctly completes both sentences.

11 Use the _____ to make the hole. The _____ team won a prize.

    Ⓕ drill   Ⓗ needle

    Ⓖ nail   Ⓙ marching

12 This _____ of plant is rare. Mr. Westgate is very _____.

    Ⓐ type   Ⓒ nice

    Ⓑ kind   Ⓓ happy

Directions: For Sample C and number 10, find the answer that best fits in the blank.

SAMPLE C Did you _____ the address in the phone book?

    Ⓐ lose   Ⓒ know

    Ⓑ find   Ⓓ forget

10 **Which word means George's project was in the center of the room?**

George's project was in the _____ of the room.

    Ⓐ front   Ⓒ middle

    Ⓑ back   Ⓓ side

Directions: For each blank, look at the words with the same number. Find the word from each list that fits best in the blank.

The bus was more __(13)__ than normal. It was raining hard, and many people who __(14)__ walked to work took the bus today.

13 Ⓕ empty   Ⓗ expensive

    Ⓖ crowded   Ⓙ practical

14 Ⓐ never   Ⓒ usually

    Ⓑ recently   Ⓓ quickly

GO

Name _____

Directions: For Sample D and numbers 15 and 16, find the part of the sentence that needs a capital letter. Mark "None" if no capital letter is needed.

SAMPLE **D**
a small bird	landed on	the feeder.	None
Ⓐ	Ⓑ	Ⓒ	Ⓓ

15
We drove	to iowa	last summer.	None
Ⓐ	Ⓑ	Ⓒ	Ⓓ

16 **Find the punctuation mark that is needed in the sentence.**   *How long will you be gone?*

.	!	,	None
Ⓕ	Ⓖ	Ⓗ	Ⓙ

Directions: Find the sentence that has correct capitalization and punctuation.

17 Ⓐ This is a great book

   Ⓑ Nora gave it to me.

   Ⓒ i'm almost done.

   Ⓓ You can have it next?

18 Ⓕ We aren't ready yet.

   Ⓖ Dont leave without us.

   Ⓗ The bags are packed? Let's go.

   Ⓙ The ride to the beach will be an hour

Directions: Read the paragraph. Find the answer that shows the correct capitalization and punctuation for the underlined parts.

(19)   *A family of <u>rabbit's visits</u> our yard every day. They eat grass and some flowers. Mom doesn't mind. She says there are plenty of flowers for*
(20)   *<u>everyone.</u> The baby rabbits seem to get bigger every day.*

19 Ⓐ rabbit's visit's   Ⓒ rabbits visits

   Ⓑ rabbits visit's   Ⓓ Correct as it is

20 Ⓕ everyone,   Ⓗ everyone!

   Ⓖ everyone?   Ⓙ Correct as it is

GO

Name _____

Directions: For each question, find the answer choice that shows correct capitalization and punctuation for the underlined words.

21 The soccer match is <u>thursday the</u> baseball game is Friday.

   Ⓐ Thursday: the   Ⓒ Thursday. the

   Ⓑ Thursday. The   Ⓓ Correct as it is

22 "What a terrifying ride that <u>was."</u> <u>Cried</u> Jake.

   Ⓕ was." Cried   Ⓗ was!" Cried

   Ⓖ was!" cried   Ⓙ Correct as it is

23 You will need the following <u>materials, Yarn,</u> scissors, cardboard, and paste.

   Ⓐ materials; yarn

   Ⓑ materials: Yarn

   Ⓒ materials: yarn

   Ⓓ Correct as it is

24 The traffic reporter <u>announced, all</u> lanes are now closed on Route 22."

   Ⓕ announced, "All

   Ⓖ announced, "all

   Ⓗ announced: "All

   Ⓙ Correct as it is

25 <u>Greensburg pennsylvania</u> is about 35 miles east of Pittsburgh.

   Ⓐ Greensburg, pennsylvania

   Ⓑ Greensburg, Pennsylvania,

   Ⓒ Greensburg, Pennsylvania

   Ⓓ Correct as it is

26 "<u>Yes, Maggie, you</u> can come over now," said Ann.

   Ⓕ "yes, Maggie, you

   Ⓖ "Yes Maggie you

   Ⓗ "Yes Maggie you,

   Ⓙ Correct as it is

27 We <u>washed dried and put</u> away the dishes.

   Ⓐ washed, dried, and put

   Ⓑ washed dried and, put

   Ⓒ washed, dried and put,

   Ⓓ Correct as it is

STOP

Test Prep

Name _____

Directions: Read the questions. Mark the letter next to the correct answer.
Use the sample index to answer numbers 28–30.

0:45
Pages 59–64
Time Limit:
approx. 45 minutes

O
Oak, 291-292
Obsidian, 175-176
Oceans, 361-375
   density of, 363-364
   life in, 367-370
   waves, 371-372
   temperature of, 365
   resources, 373-375

28 **You will find information about what topic on page 365?**

Ⓕ ocean temperatures

Ⓖ density of the ocean

Ⓗ waves

Ⓙ the octopus

29 **On what pages will you most likely find information about mining the oceans for minerals?**

Ⓐ pages 175-176

Ⓑ pages 368-369

Ⓒ pages 373-375

Ⓓ pages 371-372

30 **You can read about octopuses on pages 368-369. This information is part of what section under Oceans?**

Ⓕ resources

Ⓖ life in

Ⓗ waves

Ⓙ temperature

Directions: Use the web to answer number 31.

31 **Which of the following belongs on the web?**

Ⓐ traveling with your pet

Ⓑ heat exhaustion

Ⓒ finding a lost pet

Ⓓ cold weather and your pet

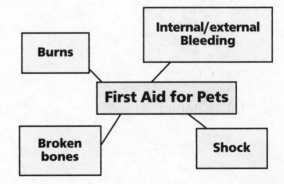

GO

Name _____

Directions: Use the sample table of contents to answer numbers 32–33.

Directions: Find the choice that rhymes with the underlined word.

Table of Contents

1 Animals Around the World 11

2 Zoos of the World 42

3 Creatures of the Sea 59

4 Rodents 85

5 Reptiles and Amphibians 101

6 Insects and Spiders 112

32 **In which chapter would you most likely read about otters, seals, and walruses?**

(F) Chapter 5

(G) Chapter 1

(H) Chapter 4

(J) Chapter 3

33 **Which chapter is the shortest?**

(A) Chapter 5

(B) Chapter 2

(C) Chapter 3

(D) Chapter 1

34 **a <u>tough</u> test**

(F) cough

(G) rough

(H) laugh

(J) thorough

35 **<u>chose</u> a new outfit**

(A) lose

(B) news

(C) close

(D) loose

36 **<u>Where</u> is the umbrella?**

(F) here

(G) were

(H) there

(J) hear

37 **the new <u>roof</u>**

(A) gruff

(B) truth

(C) wife

(D) aloof

GO

Name _____

Directions: For numbers 38–41, choose the form of the verb that correctly completes each sentence.

38 **My parents and I _____ to New York tomorrow.**

Ⓕ flew Ⓗ flies

Ⓖ are flying Ⓙ have flown

39 **My father _____ to attend a business conference.**

Ⓐ have Ⓒ having

Ⓑ haves Ⓓ has

40 **While Dad works next week, Mom and I _____ the sights.**

Ⓕ have seen Ⓗ will see

Ⓖ am seeing Ⓙ seen

41 **This time last year we _____ to San Francisco.**

Ⓐ went Ⓒ have gone

Ⓑ are going Ⓓ was going

Directions: For numbers 42–45, choose the answer choice with a usage error. If there are no errors, fill in the last answer choice.

42 Ⓕ Them cookies we baked are

Ⓖ really terrible. Even the dog wouldn't

Ⓗ eat the one I accidentally dropped.

Ⓙ no errors

43 Ⓐ The amazed children watched

Ⓑ as the doe and her fawn

Ⓒ wandered slow through the yard.

Ⓓ no errors

44 Ⓕ I could of done

Ⓖ that problem

Ⓗ without your help.

Ⓙ no errors

45 Ⓐ I gave the cookies

Ⓑ to he and she

Ⓒ because they looked angry.

Ⓓ no errors

GO

Name _____

Directions: For numbers 46–48, mark the answer choice that best combines the two sentences.

46 **Marla visited the museum today. Her sister visited the museum today.**

Ⓕ Marla and her sister visited the museum today.

Ⓖ Marla visited and her sister visited the museum today.

Ⓗ Marla visited the museum today and her sister visited the museum today.

Ⓙ Marla visited her sister and the museum today.

47 **Greg attended the concert last night. The concert was in the park.**

Ⓐ The concert last night was in the park Greg attended.

Ⓑ Greg attended last night in the park the concert.

Ⓒ Greg attended the concert last night, and the concert was in the park.

Ⓓ Greg attended the concert in the park last night.

48 **The campers watched as the bear took their food. The campers watched in horror.**

Ⓕ The campers watched as the bear took their food in horror.

Ⓖ The campers in horror watched as the bear took their food.

Ⓗ The campers watched in horror as the bear took their food.

Ⓙ The campers watched as the bear took their food, and the campers were in horror.

Directions: For numbers 49–54, mark the letter of the correctly spelled word that completes each sentence.

49 **On Saturday, I work on my _____.**

Ⓐ hobbies   Ⓒ hobies

Ⓑ hobbys   Ⓓ hobbes

50 **Your sister sings so _____ .**

Ⓕ beautifuly   Ⓗ beautifully

Ⓖ beautyfully   Ⓙ bueatifully

51 **The milk was in a _____.**

Ⓐ picher   Ⓒ pitcher

Ⓑ picture   Ⓓ pitsher

GO

Name _____

52 We are _____ up by 6:30 a.m. every morning.

   Ⓕ alwase   Ⓗ allways

   Ⓖ always   Ⓙ alwaze

53 I hope you're not_____ with your gifts.

   Ⓐ unhappy   Ⓒ unhappie

   Ⓑ unhapy   Ⓓ unhappe

54 You should always eat a good _____.

   Ⓕ brekfast

   Ⓖ breakfist

   Ⓗ breakfast

   Ⓙ brakefast

Directions: For numbers 55–60, mark the letter of the underlined word that is misspelled in each sentence. Mark the letter for no errors if all the words are spelled correctly.

55 I wouldn't be the least bit suprised if Jack got here late.   no errors
    Ⓐ   Ⓑ   Ⓒ   Ⓓ

56 Please print your name, adress, and telephone number.   no errors
    Ⓕ   Ⓖ   Ⓗ   Ⓙ

57 The choclate cake you baked is really delicious.   no errors
    Ⓐ   Ⓑ   Ⓒ   Ⓓ

58 I received an invitation to Stan's party next Saturday.   no errors
    Ⓕ   Ⓖ   Ⓗ   Ⓙ

59 Jody has been my best friend sinse we met in first grade.   no errors
                 Ⓐ   Ⓑ   Ⓒ   Ⓓ

60 We're having Thanksgiving dinner with my grandparents tomorow.   no errors
    Ⓕ   Ⓖ   Ⓗ   Ⓙ

GO

Name _____

Directions: Find the word that is spelled correctly and best fits in the blank.

61 **Let's play _____ it is nice.**

Ⓐ wheil   Ⓒ while

Ⓑ wile   Ⓓ wheil

62 **Will you _____ places with me?**

Ⓕ traid   Ⓗ traed

Ⓖ tread   Ⓙ trade

63 **An outdoor _____ is near our house.**

Ⓐ market   Ⓒ marcket

Ⓑ markit   Ⓓ marked

Directions: Find the underlined word that is not spelled correctly. If all the words are correct, mark "All correct."

64 Ⓕ <u>many</u> friends   Ⓗ feel <u>hungry</u>

Ⓖ funny <u>joke</u>   Ⓙ All correct

65 Ⓐ <u>among</u> us

Ⓑ <u>common</u> bird

Ⓒ <u>fortie</u> minutes

Ⓓ All correct

Directions: Find the answer that is the solution to the problem. If the answer is not given, choose "None of these."

66

$82 - 35 =$

Ⓕ 53

Ⓖ 47

Ⓗ 57

Ⓙ 117

Ⓚ None of these

67

$3.40
+3.60

Ⓐ $.20

Ⓑ $3.20

Ⓒ $6.00

Ⓓ $8.00

Ⓔ None of these

68

$9 \times 8 =$

Ⓕ 17

Ⓖ 64

Ⓗ 98

Ⓙ 72

Ⓚ None of these

69

305
× 6

Ⓐ 311

Ⓑ 1830

Ⓒ 3605

Ⓓ 3065

Ⓔ None of these

STOP

0:20
Time Limit:
Pages 65–68
approx. 20 minutes

Name _____

Mathematics

BUILDING OUR CLUBHOUSE

SAMPLE A — **Which of these is most likely measured in feet?**

Ⓐ the distance around a room

Ⓑ the weight of a large box

Ⓒ the distance to the moon

Ⓓ the amount of water in a pool

1 Jennie had three bent nails in her pocket. Then she put five straight nails in her pocket. Which answer shows what she had in her pocket?

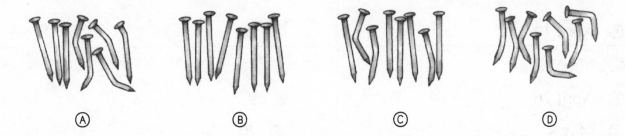

2 Ricky carried 4 boxes of tiles into the kitchen. Each box held 12 tiles. What would you do to find out how many tiles he carried into the kitchen all together?

add	subtract	divide	multiply
Ⓕ	Ⓖ	Ⓗ	Ⓙ

3 Angela wants to measure a piece of wood. Which of these should she use?

Ⓐ   Ⓑ   Ⓒ   Ⓓ

GO

Name _____

4 Mr. and Mrs. Akers are going to build a deck. It will take 2 weeks to finish. They plan to start on April 24. What date will they finish?

APRIL						
S	M	T	W	T	F	S
				1	2	3
4	5	6	7	8	9	10
11	12	13	14	15	16	17
18	19	20	21	22	23	24
25	26	27	28	29	30	

Ⓕ April 10

Ⓖ May 1

Ⓗ April 26

Ⓙ May 8

5 Pam made this pattern of 4 rows of floor tiles. How many gray tiles will she need all together if she adds 1 more row to make 5 rows of tiles?

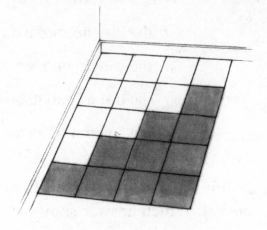

Ⓐ 5

Ⓑ 15

Ⓒ 9

Ⓓ 20

6 Which pattern of letters could be folded in half on a line of symmetry?

AMOMA	BAGGB	VERDT	UNPOS
Ⓕ	Ⓖ	Ⓗ	Ⓙ

GO

Name _____

7 The children in the Adams family were stuck inside on a rainy day. They decided to make their own games. They each made a spinner for their game. When Jennie spun her spinner, the color it landed on was gray. Which spinner was probably Jennie's?

Ⓐ
Tan
Green
Gray

Ⓒ
Tan
Green
Gray

Ⓑ
Green
Tan
Gray

Ⓓ
Gray
Green
Tan

8 This map shows Janelle's yard. She came in through the gate and walked east for 3 yards. Then she went north for 2 yards. What was she closest to?

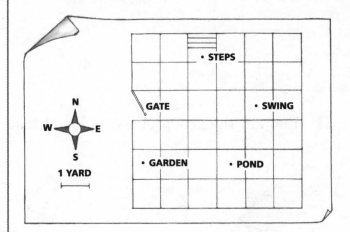

Ⓕ to the swing

Ⓖ to the pond

Ⓗ to the steps

Ⓙ to the garden

9 Rick is carving a pattern in a piece of wood. Which shapes are missing from the pattern?

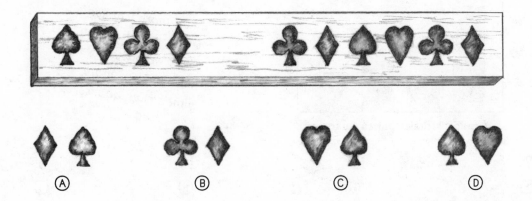

Ⓐ   Ⓑ   Ⓒ   Ⓓ

GO

Name _____

10 **Which of these is not the same shape and size as the others?**

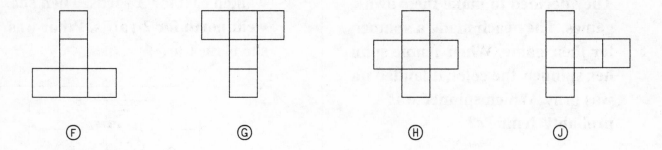

Ⓕ   Ⓖ   Ⓗ   Ⓙ

11 **Look at the group of socks. What fraction of the socks is black?**

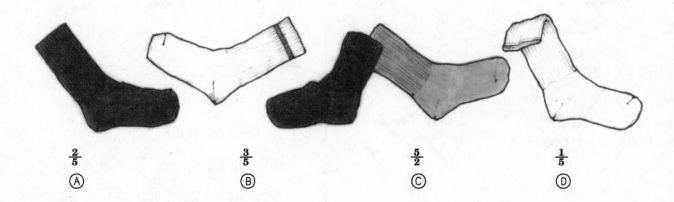

$\frac{2}{5}$ $\frac{3}{5}$ $\frac{5}{2}$ $\frac{1}{5}$
Ⓐ   Ⓑ   Ⓒ   Ⓓ

12 **Look at the graph below and the report Willie made about the coins in his change jar. How many dimes did Willie have in the change jar?**

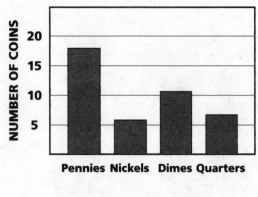

Willie's Report

I had more pennies than any other coin. There were the fewest nickels. I had more dimes than quarters.

7   11   18   6
Ⓕ   Ⓖ   Ⓗ   Ⓙ

STOP

Name _____

Directions: Choose the answer that correctly solves each problem.

0:45
Pages 69–72
Time Limit:
approx. 45 minutes

13 Which number has a 7 in the ten-thousands place and a 3 in the hundreds place?

Ⓐ 178,234   Ⓒ 498,301

Ⓑ 476,302   Ⓓ 753,092

14 What is the perimeter of the polygon?

Ⓕ 38 inches

Ⓗ 26 inches

Ⓖ 28 inches

Ⓙ not enough information

7 inches, 6 inches, 5 inches, 9 inches, 11 inches

15 Which decimal is greater than 1.32 but less than 1.41?

Ⓐ 1.42   Ⓒ 1.31

Ⓑ 1.36   Ⓓ 1.30

16 Which decimal is equal to $\frac{1}{4}$?

Ⓕ 0.25   Ⓗ 0.75

Ⓖ 0.025   Ⓙ .033

17 What could be the next number in the pattern? 3, 7, 15, 31, 63, …

Ⓐ 127   Ⓒ 96

Ⓑ 106   Ⓓ 79

18 Which animal is between 15 and 40 feet long?

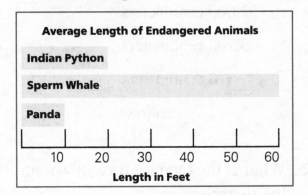

Average Length of Endangered Animals

Indian Python

Sperm Whale

Panda

10 20 30 40 50 60

Length in Feet

Ⓕ Panda   Ⓗ Indian Python

Ⓖ Sperm Whale   Ⓙ Not here

19 What other equation belongs in the same fact family as 17 × 8 = 136?

Ⓐ 8 × 136 = 1,088

Ⓑ 136 ÷ 2 = 68

Ⓒ 8 × 17 = 136

Ⓓ 17 + 8 = 25

20 Which figure shows parallel lines?

Ⓕ **S**   Ⓗ ┼

Ⓖ ═   Ⓙ ✳

GO

Name _____

21 A tsunami is a wave created by underwater earthquakes. Tsunamis can reach heights of 37 meters. How many centimeters tall is that?

Ⓐ 37,000 centimeters

Ⓑ 3,700 centimeters

Ⓒ 370 centimeters

Ⓓ 3.70 centimeters

22 What is the temperature shown on the thermometer?

Ⓕ 74° C

Ⓖ 66° C

Ⓗ 64° C

Ⓙ 54° C

23 How can you write 56,890 in expanded notation?

Ⓐ $5 + 6 + 8 + 9 + 0 =$

Ⓑ $50,000 + 6,000 + 800 + 90 =$

Ⓒ $56,000 + 8900 =$

Ⓓ $0.5 + 0.06 + 0.008 + 0.0009 =$

24 Which number is not a multiple of 4?

Ⓕ 86   Ⓗ 40

Ⓖ 68   Ⓙ 32

25 In a pictograph  stands for 5 books. How many books does

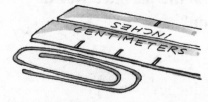

stand for?

Ⓐ 5 books   Ⓒ 20 books

Ⓑ 8 books   Ⓓ 40 books

26 How long is the paperclip?

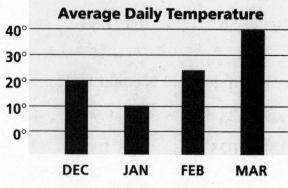

Ⓕ 3 inches   Ⓗ 3 centimeters

Ⓖ 5 inches   Ⓙ 2 centimeters

27 How much did the average daily temperature change from February to March?

Average Daily Temperature

Ⓐ 25° F   Ⓒ 10° F

Ⓑ 15° F   Ⓓ 5° F

GO

Name _____

Directions: Choose the answer that correctly solves each problem.

28 8,906 + 3,897 =

- Ⓕ 11,803
- Ⓗ 12,803
- Ⓖ 12,793
- Ⓙ 3,893

29 467.902 − 56.894 =

- Ⓐ 411.192
- Ⓒ 410.192
- Ⓑ 411.008
- Ⓓ 410.008

30 84 × .65 =

- Ⓕ 44.80
- Ⓗ 53.60
- Ⓖ 52.80
- Ⓙ 54.60

31 $\frac{3}{8} + \frac{1}{8} =$

- Ⓐ 1
- Ⓒ $\frac{4}{8}$
- Ⓑ $\frac{5}{8}$
- Ⓓ $\frac{2}{8}$

32 $\frac{279}{9} =$

- Ⓕ 3
- Ⓗ 31
- Ⓖ 26
- Ⓙ 42

33 $\frac{1}{3} + \frac{2}{3} + 1\frac{1}{3} =$

- Ⓐ $3\frac{2}{3}$
- Ⓒ 2
- Ⓑ $2\frac{1}{3}$
- Ⓓ $1\frac{1}{3}$

34 $\frac{1784}{2} =$

- Ⓕ 876
- Ⓖ 892
- Ⓗ 1,784
- Ⓙ 3,568

35 24.75 + 27.5 + 25.6 =

- Ⓐ 77.85
- Ⓑ 77.4
- Ⓒ 53.10
- Ⓓ 50.35

36 4321 + 2987 =

- Ⓕ 7,308
- Ⓖ 7,208
- Ⓗ 7,108
- Ⓙ 1,334

37 $\frac{15.05}{5} =$

- Ⓐ 3.01
- Ⓑ 3.1
- Ⓒ 31
- Ⓓ 82

GO

Name _____

Directions: Choose the answer that correctly solves each problem.

38 Michael was at a card convention. At the first booth he bought 8 cards. He bought 6 cards at each of the remaining 9 booths. How many cards did Michael buy altogether?

Ⓕ 54 cards   Ⓗ 57 cards

Ⓖ 62 cards   Ⓙ 72 cards

39 There were 85 boxes shipped to the warehouse. In each box there were 22 cartons. In each carton there were 40 water guns. How many water guns are in all 85 boxes?

Ⓐ 880 water guns

Ⓑ 1,870 water guns

Ⓒ 74,800 water guns

Ⓓ Not enough information

40 Mary measured the length of a room at 8 feet. How many inches long is the room?

Ⓕ 12 inches

Ⓖ 24 inches

Ⓗ 96 inches

Ⓙ None of these

41 Mr. Thomas bought 2 adult tickets and 1 child ticket to the amusement park. How much money did he spend altogether?

Ⓐ $44.85   Ⓒ $29.90

Ⓑ $38.85   Ⓓ $23.90

42 Rita left dance class at 3:30 p.m. She arrived home at 4:17 p.m. How long did it take Rita to get home?

Ⓕ 1 hour, 17 minutes

Ⓖ 47 minutes

Ⓗ 37 minutes

Ⓙ 13 minutes

STOP

0:15
Pages 73–74
Time Limit:
approx. 15 minutes

Name _____

Social Studies

Directions: Choose the best answer for numbers 1–6.

1 **The Boston Tea Party happened because**

Ⓐ workers didn't like to sail.

Ⓑ people believed the tax on tea was not fair.

Ⓒ bosses wanted to take a break and have fun.

Ⓓ settlers needed to move to a new town.

2 **The first President of the United States was**

Ⓕ John Adams.

Ⓖ Thomas Jefferson.

Ⓗ George Washington.

Ⓙ Abraham Lincoln.

3 **Which *probably* did not happen because of the invention of the steam engine?**

Ⓐ People visited other states more often.

Ⓑ Children had fewer school days.

Ⓒ Businesses sent their goods across the country.

Ⓓ Workers had new jobs.

4 **Who *probably* made the first United States flag?**

Ⓕ Betsy Ross

Ⓖ John Hancock

Ⓗ Benjamin Franklin

Ⓙ Dolly Madison

5 **What invention helped clean raw cotton?**

Ⓐ sewing machine

Ⓑ slaves

Ⓒ cotton gin

Ⓓ the plow

6 **What *probably* helped pioneers decide to go to California?**

Ⓕ There were big cities there.

Ⓖ There were no Indians.

Ⓗ Travel was safe and cheap.

Ⓙ Gold was discovered there.

GO

Name _____

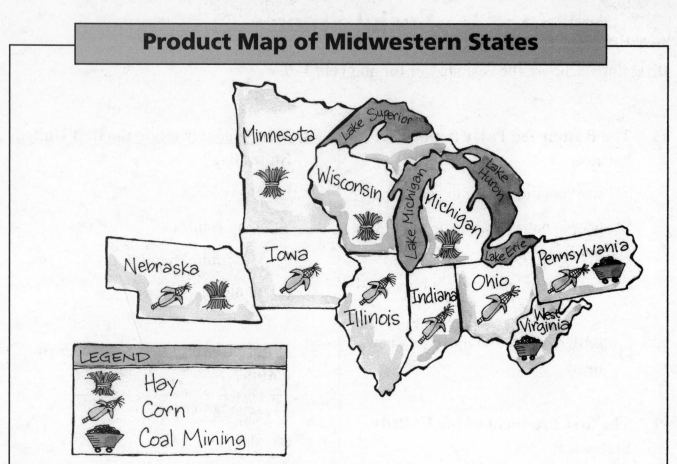

Product Map of Midwestern States

LEGEND
Hay
Corn
Coal Mining

7 **Which state does *not* grow hay?**

Ⓐ Wisconsin   Ⓒ Illinois

Ⓑ Minnesota   Ⓓ Michigan

8 **You would find coal mines in**

Ⓕ Illinois and Pennsylvania.   Ⓗ Iowa and Nebraska.

Ⓖ West Virginia and Indiana.   Ⓙ Pennsylvania and West Virginia.

9 **Which state grows both hay and corn?**

Ⓐ Ohio   Ⓒ Iowa

Ⓑ Nebraska   Ⓓ Wisconsin

STOP

0:15
Pages 75–76
Time Limit:
approx. 15 minutes

Name _____

Science

Directions: Do numbers 1–6.

1 **What kind of scientist studies rocks and minerals?**

Ⓐ biologist

Ⓑ botanist

Ⓒ archeologist

Ⓓ geologist

2 **A rock that was formed by volcanic activity is called**

Ⓕ sedimentary.

Ⓖ igneous.

Ⓗ metamorphic.

Ⓙ mineral.

3 **A sedimentary rock is often formed in a**

Ⓐ river bed.

Ⓑ volcano.

Ⓒ mesa.

Ⓓ plateau.

4 **A scientist scratches a mineral sample with her fingernail, a penny, and then a nail. What property is she testing?**

Ⓕ shininess

Ⓖ chemical make-up

Ⓗ weight

Ⓙ hardness

5 **The outermost layer of the Earth is called the**

Ⓐ outer core.

Ⓑ inner core.

Ⓒ crust.

Ⓓ mantle.

6 **A sudden movement of the Earth's crust is known as**

Ⓕ a volcano.

Ⓖ an earthquake.

Ⓗ a hurricane.

Ⓙ a tornado.

GO

Name _____

Directions: Read the diagram, and then do numbers 7 and 8.

Before   **After**

7   **Which principle is shown in the diagram?**

(A) evaporation

(B) displacement

(C) metamorphosis

(D) isolation

8   **What would happen if the rock in Picture 2 were small instead of large?**

(F) The water level would be higher.

(G) The water would have evaporated.

(H) The water level would be lower.

(J) The water level would be the same.

Directions: Read the graph, and then do numbers 9 and 10.

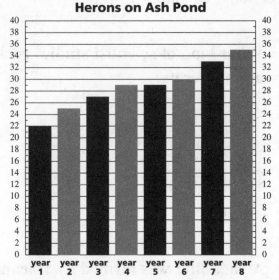

Herons on Ash Pond

9   **In which two years did the number of herons stay the same?**

(A) years 1 and 2

(B) years 2 and 3

(C) years 3 and 4

(D) years 4 and 5

10   **Based on the data, what could you predict for year 11?**

(F) The number of herons will increase.

(G) The number of herons will decrease.

(H) The number of herons will stay the same.

(J) Herons will become endangered.

STOP

Grade 3 Answer Key

Page 15
  A. B
  B. F

Page 17
  1. C
  2. F

Page 18
  3. B
  4. H
  5. C
  6. F
  7. B

Page 20
  8. F
  9. C

Page 21
  10. J
  11. B
  12. H

Page 22
  A. A
  1. A
  2. H

Page 23
  3. A
  4. G
  5. C
  6. F
  7. B

Page 24
  8. J
  9. B
  10. F
  11. C
  12. F
  13. D

Page 25
  Responses will vary.

Page 26
FIRST QUESTION: Possible response: It is Juan. He is nervous about seeing his friend, because he hasn't seen him in 6 months.

SECOND QUESTION: Possible response: The story doesn't say where the story takes place. It doesn't really matter.

THIRD QUESTION: Possible response: He is afraid that it won't be the same, but the friend puts him at ease.

Page 27
  A. A
  1. A
  2. G
  3. B
  4. J

Page 28
  A. B
  B. F
  1. A
  2. J
  3. C
  4. F
  5. C

Page 29
  C. B
  6. D
  7. F
  8. A
  9. J

Page 30
  A. B
  1. A
  2. H
  B. C
  3. C
  4. J

Grade 3 Answer Key

Page 31
5. D
6. H
C. B
7. C
8. J

Page 32
1. A
2. J
3. B
4. G
5. C
A. D
6. B
7. J
8. C

Page 33
A. C
B. K
1. D
2. K
3. A
4. G

Page 34
A. C

Page 35
1. B
2. F
3. D
4. F
5. B

Page 36
6. F
7. D
8. F
9. B
10. F
11. C

Page 37
12. F
13. B
14. J

Page 38
15. D
16. J
17. A

Page 39
1. B
2. F
3. D

Page 40
4. G
5. C
6. F
7. B

Page 41
1. C
2. G
3. A
4. H

Page 42
5. B
6. H
7. B
8. H
9. A
10. F
11. D

Page 43
A. A

Page 44
1. C
2. F
3. B
4. J

Page 45
5. A
6. H
7. B

Page 46
8. J
9. C
10. F
11. B

Page 47
12. G
13. C

Page 48
14. F
15. A
16. H
17. A
18. H

Grade 3 Answer Key

Page 49
19. B
20. H
21. D
22. B
23. A
24. B
25. A

Page 50
26. H
27. B
28. J
29. B

Page 51
30. J
31. D
32. H
33. A
34. H

Page 52
35. D
36. F
37. C
38. G
39. C
40. A
41. B
42. D
43. G
44. J
45. F
46. H

Page 53
Responses will vary.

Page 54
Responses will vary.

Page 55
A. B
1. A
2. G
3. A
4. G
5. A
6. H
7. D

Page 56
B. D
8. B
9. G
C. B
10. C
11. F
12. B
13. G
14. C

Page 57
D. A
15. B
16. J
17. B
18. F
19. C
20. J

Page 58
21. B
22. G
23. C
24. H
25. C
26. J
27. A

Page 59
28. F
29. C
30. G
31. B

Page 60
32. G
33. A
34. G
35. C
36. H
37. D

Page 61
38. G
39. D
40. H
41. A
42. F
43. C
44. F
45. B

Page 62
46. F
47. D
48. H
49. A
50. H
51. C

Grade 3 Answer Key

Page 63
52. G
53. A
54. H
55. C
56. G
57. A
58. J
59. B
60. H

Page 64
61. C
62. J
63. A
64. J
65. C
66. G
67. E
68. J
69. B

Page 65
A. A
1. C
2. J
3. B

Page 66
4. J
5. A
6. F

Page 67
7. A
8. H
9. D

Page 68
10. H
11. A
12. G

Page 69
13. B
14. F
15. B
16. F
17. A
18. H
19. C
20. G

Page 70
21. B
22. H
23. B
24. F
25. D
26. H
27. B

Page 71
28. H
29. B
30. J
31. C
32. H
33. B
34. G
35. A
36. F
37. A

Page 72
38. G
39. C
40. H
41. B
42. G

Page 73
1. B
2. H
3. B
4. F
5. C
6. J

Page 74
7. C
8. J
9. B

Page 75
1. D
2. G
3. A
4. J
5. C
6. G

Page 76
7. B
8. H
9. D
10. F